A Lyrical Collective

Volume I

Neil J. McKenzie

A LYRICAL COLLECTIVE
VOLUME I

iUniverse books may be ordered through booksellers or by contacting:

iUniverse
1663 Liberty Drive
Bloomington, IN 47403
www.iuniverse.com
1-800-Authors (1-800-288-4677)

ISBN: 978-1-5320-8400-3 (sc)
ISBN: 978-1-5320-8401-0 (e)

Library of Congress Control Number: 2019914654

Print information available on the last page.

iUniverse rev. date: 10/31/2019

Dedicated to all my friends and family who put up with my proof readings and crazy ideas. They gave me the inspiration to write this book and the next two volumes. Dedicated to Gillian Mckenzie, "Eddie Clay" and the "Calfornia Executives" especially, my beautiful daughter, Kayla P. Love you.

Contents

"Spirit of the Wolf"

Blue Cloud knew she had but one
chance to make her arrow count
She made it up the backside of the
hill before she left her mount
The spirit of the wolf was strong inside her
she could see the silhouette of her prey
She hoped her ancestors would guide her
hand to a target fifty yards away
This is what stood between her and her
tribe, the last of her Indian clan
She knew she was chosen to provide for her
people and if she missed, they would surely die
She let fly the arrow it flew like a sparrow
as it disappeared through the mist
She heard the sound of the buffalo hitting the ground
Then she dropped to her knees in prayer.

(By Neil Mckenzie)

"Pathfinder"

Pathfinder was exhausted but it was almost dawn
He found the trail of the buffalo but they had already
moved on.
Blue Cloud had told him he must perform the dance.
The dance of the buffalo if he wanted any chance.
The snow had started to fall and the trail would be gone.
But the spirit of the wolf had never steered him wrong.
He found the tracks of the great white wolf who was
taking long strides...
He must have caught scent of the herd.
He was heading straight for the rise...
Through the meadow and across the river he chased
his canine brother.
He came to a spot where he could look out and survey
the entire area.
And there they were, at least a thousand in the herd.
They were covered in snow and traveling in one
single row.
He then stopped to whisper a prayer
so he could thank the mighty creator for a hunt well
done.

(By Neil Mckenzie)

"Pathfinder part II"

He then saw something, it enraged and terrified him
all at the same time.
A party of Buffalo skinners ready to perform their
sacrilegious crime.
Pathfinder took off running towards the men.
All he knew was they just performed a sin.
He was deadset on making them pay for their evil
deed.
The hunters had all discharged their weapons, so they
decided their was no need.
But when they saw Pathfinder and the Wolf Clan, it
was time for them to run.
Too late for a truce...
Talking was of no use...
They headed across the frozen lake in an extreme
haste.
They picked up their trophies and fled without waste.
The weight of the skins had loaded them down, and
they fell through the ice barely making a sound.
The Wolf Clan stopped and began their song.
They thanked the creator for punishing this wrong.

(By Neil Mckenzie)

"The Sundance part 1"

Blue Cloud felt she was being watched
As she and Pathfinder ascended the rocks
They had reached the sacred, "Mountain to the Sun"
But they had to climb to the top before they were
done
This was the home of the great mountain cats
Protectors of the ancestral burial grounds
Defenders of the Sun Dance altars and traditions
Pathfinder knew this was a very dangerous mission
He also summoned the guardian of the night
In the early hours of the dawn you could see traces of
his light
He was the first Pathfinder, his mighty ancestor
He would deliver the message from the first nations
creator
When it was time, the 4 eagles would take flight and
show the sign to his people before the days light
The clan of the wolf would be stronger than ever
With the Sun Dance complete and their faith beyond
measure

(By Neil Mckenzie)

"The Sun Dance part ll"

The blood thirsty scream of the big mountain cat
Caused them both to freeze right in their tracks
It echoed throughout the hills and the floor of the
canyon letting all to know their actions should be
abandoned
Blue Cloud whispered, "we must move on..."
"They surely know why we are here so don't run..."
As they reached the top of the platau rim
They heard a growl, a roar and a hiss from within
It was a huge mountain cat the biggest she had ever
seen
Its eyes were two piercing lights that were emerald
green
You could see the massive power in this brawny cats
claws
It was the perfect killing machine, the killers of all
Then suddenly they heard the howl of a distant wolf
The cry of an eagle
And the rustling in the brush
She knew the cats were ready, ready to kill men
But the spirit of the wolf was not at its end

(By Neil Mckenzie)

"The Sun Dance part lll"

The sound from the brush came closer and closer
Louder and louder their hearts pounding faster and
harder
Then it broke through the thicket in one explosive
shot
It was god-like as it stood on its hind legs on the rock
It was the Great One
The powerful Grizzly
The beast of the cave
He had no fear
He was the alpha male
His intent was very clear
His roar was deafening
But it was all for show
He was friend to the wolf clan and not their foe.
Behind the great one came the clan of the wolf
It was a pack of 4 canines who came as fast as they
could
The lions were on edge since they were protecting
their cubs
But when they saw the wolf clan, thats when they
understood.

It was time for the great ceremony, the dance of the sun
The 4 eagles took flight for their sacred nocturnal run.

(By Neil Mckenzie)

"The Sun Dance part IV Epilogue"

Blue clouds vision was finally complete
She and Pathfinder had brought faith to their peoples
feet
The time of sadness had come to an end
The time of prosperity and happiness was about to
begin
It took all the creatures of the mountain to get all the
elements aligned
It took the spirit of the wolf clan to save them just in
time
They were the last survivors of the massacre of Indian
Pass
The 4 nations leaders had perished with no chance
It was Blue Cloud and Pathfinder who united all the
tribes
It was the Wolf Clan and their ancestors who gave
them the hope to survive.
The End...

(By Neil Mckenzie)

"Legend of the White Buffalo" (part I).

The village was starving, there was no food to be
found
Children were crying while old ones dropped dead to
the ground
Two hunters were tasked to find their people some
game
"Please come back with meat to avoid this terrible
shame"
They came to a hill and looked to the other side
They saw a beautiful maiden, she floated as she could
glide
Now one hunter approached her, he wanted to fulfill
his evil needs
The other one said stop! We have a village we have to
feed !
As he touched the woman, his body was set to flames
He then exploded everywhere nothing but old bones
were left to claim
The other hunter decided it was time for him to run
The woman said stop i have a prophecy of good and
bad things to come....
(Poem by Neil Mckenzie)
Story of the Lakota

"Legend of the White Buffalo (part II)

The hunter returned to the village to explain what he
had just seen
He told of the blessing and the warning they would
receive
He told of the great meeting that was about to
convene
She then appeared 4 days later, floating just over the
horizon
In a white buckskin dress singing in the Lakota
tongue
I will teach you the seven rites, your first lesson has
just begun
She told them she was a holy woman from the great
Buffalo Nation
Her medicine was to lead the people from this great
devastation
She gave them the pipe, it was a sacred communicator
It was a gift from the nations true first creator
She said we were related to all creatures of the land
And we were connected to the Buffalo, sacred beast
to the red man...
(Poem by Neil Mckenzie)

"Legend of the White Buffalo" (part III)

"With visible breath i am walking" she told the
Lakota people
She then transformed into a buffalo calf who began to
change its colorful features
From black to red to yellow to white
I will return to see if your path is right
My spirit will never travel beyond your heart
So follow the buffalo it will make a good start
I am "white buffalo calf woman"
I leave you with a good omen
She vanished inside a herd of buffalo that surrounded
the villiage encampment
My gift to the Lakota and all red men
The buffalo will always be your sacred friend
(Poem by Neil Mckenzie)

"The Valley of Death"

This woman had been abandoned by her own wagon
train
The thought of Cholera was racing through her veins
The Indians stayed away, fearing for the worst
Thinking that this "Bruja" would cast an evil curse
So she lived alone in the forest called "The Valley of
Death"
Surviving with the beast's and shunned by the rest
She hunted with an owl and the Clan of the Wolf
Her family were the animals, but she depended on
herself...
(Poem by Neil Mckenzie)

"Wolf Clan" (The Intruders)

The wolf clan signaled remain perfectly still
There was danger approaching from the other side of
the hill
She always trusted their acute sense of instinct
So she reacted quickly before she could even think
A hunting party entered the Valley of Death
As they approached slowly, the woman held her
breath
The wolf clan sent a warning, three yelps and a howl
Then suddenly the whole valley joined in with a
massive growl
The hunters dropped their weapons and fled for their
lives
They were in the land of the "Bruja" to stay was
unwise...
(By Neil Mckenzie)

"The Manifest Destiny"

The Manifest Destiny such a noble term...
It was just an excuse for conquering, then
moving on...
It betrayed the Red, Black and Mexican man...
It killed, enslaved or pushed him off his land...
It was powered by greed and the American need...
To keep big capitolists and politics free...
When the indians wouldnt go, they decided to wipe
out the Buffalo...
"Let them move to Canada to eat"...
When that didnt work they really became jerks and
gave them diseased blankets and rotten meat...
"We will get that gold no matter what !"...
"And the South shall rise again"...
These phrases just blew up in their faces as one of the
greatest losses of men.

(By Neil Mckenzie)

"The Color of the Soul"

You all look, but you don't see
We all bare the fruit from the same sacred tree
Some are light and some are dark
We all were protected by the strength of our mothers
bark
Our mission in life was just to survive
But collectively, our species will thrive
All our seeds, they appear to be the same
It takes the miracle of life to give an individual name
We live our lives until we are dead
If you look at whats inside of us, you will see our
blood is red
The blessed ones will love beyond old
Do you think their spirit cares about "The Color of
the Soul?"

(By Neil Mckenzie)

"The Blueprint"

Dr. Martin Luther King
What an incredible human being...
After he told the people of his magnificent dream, he
told the children of a blueprint for developing their
theme...
Do not fear who you are...
Do not fear what you look like...
Be proud of your race...
You are not a disgrace...
Be the architech...
What a great metaphor...
It starts with dignity determination freedom and
justice for all...
Be the best you can while helping your fellow man...
In reality...
What if this was in every nations plan?

(By Neil Mckenzie)

"Harriet Tubman"

Harriet Tubman... simply known as "Moses"...
She lead her people to the promised land... time and time again...
She was an escaped slave who had been beaten in her day...
But she used the underground railroad to show our people the way...
She also was an Army scout that lead the Union on a raid...
They freed 700 slaves that day but she new there were more lives to save...
Mission after mission she continued to cross the line...
A warrior for the people, there was no finer soldier you could find...
Some of our people they just didnt know...
If they knew they were slaves...
Harriet would have had a thousand more trips to go...

(By Neil Mckenzie)

"Frederick Douglas"

Frederick Douglas, a man among men...
Born a slave...
But became the greatest civil rights leader of his day...
He fought as an abolitionist...
He fought against slavery...
He fought for womens sufferage...
He wouldnt let anything get in his way...
He was nominated as a candidate for Vice President
of these United States...
I wonder if he had won...
Would he have suffered Lincoln's fate?
He would grab the American conscience in the
attempt to educate...
Then release the "Fire and Brimstone" to agitate,
agitate agitate...

(By Neil Mckenzie)

"Liberty"

Give me your tired, your poor, your huddled masses...
These are
the words that rang true with so much compassion...
So they use the term, "The Brown Invasion"...
I guess it doesnt work for this somber ocassion.
Some say he is fulfilling a political agenda...
What about ethics and humanity for our moreno
persuasion?...
Maybe progress will be made on Capitol Hill...
But its already too late for the ones who lay still..
(By Neil Mckenzie)

"The Gun"

A gun is like a tool, that can be used by any old fool.
It has no state of mind.
It will take a special person that has to be properly
chosen to deal with not committing a crime.
If you have a problem dont choose a weapon, choose
your brain its the most powerful thing.
Be a man, take a stand and come up with a plan.
Diplomacy goes a lot further than you think.
Don't be a punk and just grab your junk.
And end the life of an innocent bystander.
The true gift, is not to cause a rift and win in the
meetings of the mind.
Now i have to ask, if your not up to the task
And your heart is so cold.
That you have no soul.
Put that gun in your hand, and just end it man...
"We aint got time for your martyr roles".

(By Neil Mckenzie)

"Dirty Diana and the Pirates of the Black Falcon" part 1

She had the clue to find the treasure...
Only she could lead them to wealth beyond measure...
This creature could never be trusted...
It was the cause of her entire crew getting busted...
She had to rely on the speed of the Black Falcon...
It was the only ship that could catch up to Sir Edward Malcom...
He was protected by the entire Britsh Navy...
But Diana had a bold plan...
It was a great risk...
And her crew thought she was crazy...

(By Neil Mckenzie)

"Dirty Diana and the Pirates of the Black Falcon" (part II)

Now the Black Falcon was the fastest ship to sail the seven seas...

With a full wind in her sails, she could bring any battleship to their knee's...

Dirty Diana could easily catch up to the ship, but to surprise-attack them that was the trick...

So she disguised the Falcon as an old cargo boat...

But once they got closer, she was able to flip the script on this dangerous joke...

(By Neil Mckenzie)

"Dirty Diana and the Pirates of the Black Falcon" (part III)

Ahoy you bastards !!! youre out-gunned and out-matched !!!

This is Captain Diana, i will blow you to hell and back !!!

Prepare to be boarded by the Black Falcons crew, you had better cooperate if you know whats good for you...

I'm Dirty Diana and I mean what I say...

You better give up that map if you want to live to see another day !!!

Sir Malcom scurried up topside as he pissed in his pants...

Dirty Diana snatched his map without giving him a glance...

If it werent for you, i would still have my crew...

So i'm pissed off and i'll tell you what i'm gonna do...

I'll burn your sails and confiscate your weapons...

I will set you adrift until you reach the Chinese nation...

You took my "Naughty Neil", the best man i ever had...

I'm gonna cut off your balls and ears, then fly them under my pirates flag...

(By Neil Mckenzie)

"Dirty Diana and the Pirates of the Black Falcon" (part IV)

As Dirty Diana slowly raised her bloody sword..
She said, "Malcom, do you have any final words?"...
As we executed your crew two by two, it was yours
and Naughty Neil's turn for the queen to review...
Dont worry about Neil he is alive and well...
He violated the queen now she's under his spell...
She wanted to crown him king, a real royal being.
So he talked her into sparing your life amongst other
things...
She thought it was proper to set him free until he
made off with the Crown Jewels as he started to flee...
He went in search of you to find his true love...
He mentioned a secret place called the "Pirates
Cove"...
On the "Island of the Double Heart"...
We couldnt find it on any chart...
Its connected to this map, so you know where he's at...
Now can you please spare my ears and balls, since ive
confessed to everything i could recall?
Diana's heart returned to its proper place and a
beautiful smile came upon her face...
Set sail for the Island of the Double Heart...
♥Neil already has a pretty good start...

She took her sword and ran Malcom through...
"You weasel"...
"This is pay-back for killing my crew"...

(By Neil Mckenzie)

"Path of the warrior"

Peabody Slamm was a changed man, you could see it
in his eyes
He wasnt with the law cause they had too many flaws
So he chose his own way to die
He had gone full ronin just like the shoguns, none of
his clients survived
If you ask him for the reason, depending on the
season, he'd say," just waitin to die".
His weapons of choice were his knife and tai chi
Those who witnessed never lived to disagree
He was so fast and so quick, they were dead within a
click
Thank God he never came after me.

(By Neil Mckenzie)

"The Pub"

As Mr. Slamm slid into one of his favorite pubs, he realized he hadnt eaten in two days...
"I'll have the house special "...
Let me have bacon, peanut butter and turkey...
With a side of Jack and coke please...
Extra lettuce but hold the cheese..
As he wolfed down his sandwich he decided it was time to light up...
A filterless Camel would be the perfect touch...
Then from behind him he heard "Sir theres no smoking in here !"
Instantly there was silence and the room began to clear...
Slamm turned around and said "Oh what a treat !"...
She was beautiful, she was security and he could tell she was in heat...
As she made the move to cuff me, i countered with a dose of positve chi...
She dropped to her knees, "What did you do?!!"...
Her blouse was covered in sweat...
And her trousers were all wet...
"All i saw was a flash of red and white, then i experienced some kind of sexual delite !"

As he lifted her up, he said as a joke...
"It would have lasted longer if you let me finish my smoke."

(By Neil Mckenzie)

"Tao of Peabody Slamm"

Peabody Slamm the ladys man, he played the freaks,
the best in the land
But his mission in life was to find himself a wife
One he could treat as his equal
So from dusk to noon all the ladies he would swoon
One by one he would please them
Then one day as she started to walk away
He said "Eureka" i found her !!!
So Peabody Slamm became the happiest man because
he thought he found his pot of gold
But little did he know, she was cut from his mold and
a little sex would not please her...
So he stood in line and waited the time
Until his wife cried,
"Your turn player !"

(By Neil Mckenzie)

"House of Whack"

When i was a little boy, not too long ago
My momma told me never fall in love with the first
girl that i saw
Well i thought twice but i took her advice and then i
shuffled right out the door
I went to the party where the women party hardy and
the fellas just beg for more

I was in like flynn so let the party begin theres a
party in the house of whack
Its where all the freaks and mighty fine girls try to
front like theyre better than that
Well i dove in like a natural man can cause i thought i
had something to prove
I started bumpin and a jumpin and a foolin around
until the floor couldnt take my groove
But she was in the mood....
I was in her groove.......

About 3 days later, it might have been 4 that i finally
crawled out of the Whack
I was drained, beaten and brutally malled as i laid on
my back

Oh theres a morale to this story cause it had to be told
about this infamous house of whack
Be care what you wish for, be careful what you get
Theres an ugly little secret hiding in the Whack
But she was in the mood....
I was in her groove....

(By Neil Mckenzie)

"You're under arrest" From the Tao of Slamm

It started out one muggy day while most at work i at play
I chanced to glance with shifty eyes that luscious girl
with the pretty eyes
I had to have her for my own, so i knocked her out
just to take her home
I got as far as fifth and third when ears picked up
these funny words
Two plain clothed cops were doggin me
When one said halt the other freeze !

You're under arrest....4X

So before the judge he had to stand the toughest in
the country for this reprimand
But he was walkin tall, talkin stuff he could handle
all these powder puffs.
Well im a natural man raised on the streets
My momma was a slut and my daddy a thief
I lived all these years doin as i please
When i saw the girl i knew she was for me..

Well youre a product of the ghetto i must confess you
got problems with ethics and your lifes a mess

I gonna "slamm" you hard son with all my might, oh
you can beg and plead but thats alright

You're under arrest ...4X

So years and years dragged on by, as i served my
sentence i thought id die
Then it came that inevitable date they opened the
door that pearly gate
So i walked the streets a reborn man until i saw that
raging hand
That savage scene that girl in trouble it was my life
only in double

So i broke his back with one quick swing
I thought to myself its the proper thing
As i picked her up from this bloody cover
She took to me like a new found lover
I took her home as quick as i could i spoke to her
softly as a lover would
She turn to say a passionate line when two shots hit
me dead from behind
She screamed in pity and began to cry
Little did she know i was her "First" shifty guy

"A New Dawn"

I never took her seriously, what she might do...
I never believed her when she said we were through...
I always took for granted that she would always be there
My heart was devastated when I couldnt find her anywhere...
When her lips would move, I would never hear...
When she was crying i never noticed the tears
It's me now, down on my knees...
Sick to my stomach begging god please...
I'm so sorry I treated her like trash...
But like the phoenix she rose from the ash
In her note, she said today was a new dawn
Now I know what it feels like to have a broken heart torn.

(By Neil Mckenzie)
Artist Zig Wharton

"The Marines"

As the hypnotic sound of the chopper fills your ears...
It produces a calmness to balance the battle thats
pending near...
Various thoughts race through each Marines mind...
But its the mission and its execution is what you will
find...
Because they know without this...
There will be no true path to return to the ones they
miss...
Pride, training and Espirit de Corps is what keeps
these Marines coming back for more...
With the final pitch of the blade, these stray thoughts
begin to fade...
Boots on the ground is the task at hand...
You are the ultimate battle plan...
"Its time to kick ass and take names !"
"We are the United States Marines !!!"

(By Neil Mckenzie)

"Sasquatch"

Some say he's a hideous beast with a gleam in
his eye...
He rarely leaves a track, but you can sometimes hear
his cry...
He smells of death but its just a warning to you...
Beware of wood knocks and pole crosses too.
They say he can toss a stone twice as big as your head,
and snap a tree trunk as thick as his leg...
Do you really want to find him?...
Are you really that bold?...
I honestly think, you should just leave him alone...
You want to find his bones? Thats easy to do...
They are resting with the "Mound Builders"... thats
your clue...
7 to 18 foot tall, just to name a few...
Unless he was confiscated by a Smithsonian
archeological crew...
Native Americans, Vikings, Lewis and Clark, they
knew...
Megellan, Desoto, Washington, Roosevelt and
Lincoln too...

I think the biggest mystery is not discovering a new race...
But the huge cover-up that would make government and science lose face...

(By Neil Mckenzie)

"The Command Performance"

She lights up the stage like no diva can
She controls the band with a slight movement of her
hand
The crowd roars in an imminant anticipation of a
command performance with a driving sensation
Her beauty is matched only by the sound of her voice
Its clear to me, shes the peoples choice
So stand for the show that will blow you away, its the
thrill of a lifetime you will see this day.

(By Neil Mckenzie)

"The Music Man"

Softly falling like a springtime rain.
His music flows throughout his veins.
Without effort, nor thought or care.
With ease comes words he holds so dear.
He hones his craft to the tee.
Making it perfect for you and me.
A beautiful tone ready to start.
A full house with a beat in their hearts.
He's here to set the crowd on fire.
He lites them up, taking them higher and higher.
With a burst of love and a beautiful melody.
Creating a sound so unique and varying.
By nights end they will know his claim.
He will make your soul dance without knowing your
name.

(By Dee Jones/Neil Mckenzie)

"The Dharma Wheel"

From the 4th noble truth spins the spokes of the
Dharma wheel...
With the tools of the "Right" Insight...
Nirvana and Wisdom shall yield...
This eight-fold journey is essential for the Buddhist
foundation...
From Moral virtues to meditation...
These were the goals of its early creation...
Dharma is the cosmic law and order that Buddha
used back in his day...
With a hub, spoke, rim and a spin...
He simply called it "The Middle Way".

(By Neil Mckenzie)

"The Noble Truths"

The Noble Truths they will set you free
Its the Ideology of life how it should be
There are only 4, but they will have to do
The subject is "Suffering" from me to you
To put it in its proper sequence, we will have to place
it on a philosophical fence
Pain is a sign of life can be one
2 is a head full of selfish ambition
Nirvana is the sign that your desires can be overcome
The 4th is the path of an eight-fold journey for some
These are basic goals for any Buddhist looking in...
But to follow these truths, would fit any of man's
religions...

(By Neil Mckenzie)

"Yin Yang"

When your feeling down and your spirit is in trouble
Just reach deep within your soul there is a balance
point level
It protects the good from the bad
The glad from the sad
The love from the hate
Use your strength its your fate
To defeat what gives you a fright
To run it may seem alright
But the power is yours
To defeat all those flaws
You can do it my friend
Just battle to the end
I know you can hang
With the balance of
"Yin Yang"

(By Neil Mckenzie)

"Life is Too Short"

Life's too short, the time is now
Reasons of insanity will hold you down
Negative people will harvest your drive, while positive
ones will help you to strive
Stay on point to achieve success
Dont veer from the goal to get involved in a mess
Help the ones whose heart is true
Ignore the ones who have no faith in you
Try to be fair in all your endeavors
Bottom line, your rep is your measure.

(By Neil Mckenzie)

"The Predator"

This scene had been played since the dawn of time...
A predator against a mother protecting her kind...
He sized her up and smelled the fear...
But it was smothered by his overconfidence since they
were trapped in his lair...
She had one thing on her mind, to protect her
young...
Mother's instinct said it was beyond the time to run...
He paused to make his deadly move...
She crouched to brace herself, it was all she could do...
Then she extended her claws as she tore at his chest...
She caught his throat then ripped out the rest...
He knew his time was through, since his jugular was
torn and sliced in two...
She paused to let out a primal scream...
She turned and said...
"Mommy's sorry this man was so mean."

(By Neil Mckenzie)

"The Carnivore"

Two packs of ferocious carnivores surrounded the
wounded offspring...
With tension in the air and blood everywhere not sure
how this battle would fare...
Then out jumped the alpha female, she was old,
haggard and scarred...
What she lacked in size and strength, she gained in
tactics above par...
The subdominant males all tucked in their tails
knowing they could be collateral damage...
Then from behind a tree, their female leader stepped
free ready to partake in this skirmish...
They circled each other again and again..
Not quite sure when this battle would begin...
Then the old one took a bite of the others ear...
Then she ripped it off without showing any fear...
"If you want to play soccer in the Bronx"...
"You gotta watch for the goalie throwing rocks !!!"

(By Neil Mckenzie)

"Think of me"

Think of me, as your inspiration...
Think of me as the one who really cares...
Call my name when your down and in trouble...
Im your friend, the best thats ever been...
I will give you hope when you only have desire...
I will be that spark when you really need a fire...
I offer love, trust and friendship...
I give you hope, bond and kinship...
Your thoughts are deep within my heart...
A place where true friendship will always start...
(By Neil Mckenzie)

"The Affair"

Anger without trust stirs up revengeful lust...
It caused my mind and body to stray...
In this forbidden state of mind...
There was only one thing i wanted to find...
I didn't care about her feelings...
I was running on animal instinct to negotiate these dealings...
I stopped in a club, i didn't care who she was...
I wanted to find a girl who was willing...
After the deed, and I satisfied my need...
A cloud of darkness settled upon me...
I had to rush home... Didn't bother to phone...
Thats when i found her in bed with my brother.
I couldnt be mad at this little freak...
A good time is all he ever would seek...
He never had any virtues or morales...
As i caught my breath and took a moment to rest...
Thats when we decided it was time to talk things over.

(By Neil Mckenzie)

"Fall in Love With My Soul Tonite"

My body will grow old and die...
So fall in love wirh my soul tonite
Our bond will continue to thrive
Long after the physical ceases to survive
I believe in my heart this is true, because my soul only
has eyes for you
Our love will last forever...
Because it is a bond of universal measure
What ever you touch i will feel
When ever you pray i will kneel
If your heart feels its time to cry
That is when a part of me will die
When you are happy and need to smile...
I'll be there to celebrate for a while
I love you girl with all my might...
So fall in love with my soul tonite
(By Neil Mckenzie)

"Elements of Love"

Trust, respect and honesty
This is what love really means to me
Nothing fake inspired by your sexual drive
Something real spoken from your heart and mind
When you look deep into her eyes and you see her
soul begin to rise
You know its time to stop playing the game
And put the face of love into the frame
Most women can tell if your heart is true
Most women know if their love is for you
So if you play the game and shoot from the hip
Most of the time thats when they trip
The elements of love
My gift to you
The elements of love
They will see you through
With my heart in hand
Down on bended knee
Our hearts will combine like true love should be

(By Neil Mckenzie)

"One Step Beyond"

Have enough trust to love me...
Love me enough to trust me...
Hold my hand again...
I will be more than just your friend...
Its your beauty that atttacts me...
Its your soul that fascinates me...
But its your heart that captured me...
And your love that compels me...
Together we can be a team...
With our love, we can conquer anything...
Together, all our dreams will come true...
All i have to do, is just be with you...
Such a brilliant mind you have, my dear...
But its your determination, that will take us
anywhere...
The strength is in our bond...
Our future starts ...
With just one step beyond...

(By Neil Mckenzie)

"Destiny"

When she smiled at me, I had no clue...
I just thought she was being polite, you know how
they do...
Then the next time I passed her by...
She offered a flower... she had a gleam in her eye...
I said for me? Whats this for?
She said i don't know where you live, but i'm
knocking at your door.
Is your heart so busy it doesnt have time to explore a
new friendship with a woman who just wants to dine?
Being very apprehensive I said lets have lunch at the
beach...
She said sure as long as its my treat.
Being a little confused i agreed to the task...
Maybe she thought i was her Prince just wearing an
ugly mask.
She was beautiful she was charming she was all those
things...
She is what a man looks for just before he gives her a
ring...
I had so much fun, can we do this again?
She said my flight leaves in an hour, this is where it
ends...
The treatments not working...

I have less than a year.
You can call me "Destiny"...
I will always be near...

(By Neil Mckenzie)

"Enjoy the View"

Enjoy the view
But her heart is not for you
She is the lady in red
Dont let her smile go to your head.
She's not what you think.
So dont be fooled by a wink.
She is charming, witty and kind.
Fickled with a beautiful mind.
She is the girl
That will rule your world.
So fellas be nice or she will turn cold as ice.
Dedicated to family, friends and kin.
Happy Birthday Girl !!
It's Juliet Holleran !!!

(By Neil Mckenzie)

"Stay Strong my Queen"

If love were money...
I'd Make You a millionaire
I know you want to be strong
I freely give it without a care
Trying to survive is something we all must do
But your heart is in pain.
This is the right thing to do
I will give you my love, all that i have
To give you the strength so let evil beware
So with my love comes a strong dose of hope
This may be all you need to climb this slippery slope
So stay strong my queen
I am all that you need
Stay strong for me
I will keep your spirit free
I wont tie you down like an anchor to a boat
You will soar like an eagle as the angels take note.

(By Neil Mckenzie)

"The Dancer"

Her balance is amazing
Her form is impecable
Her dedication to the dance is nothing short of
incredible
Her stance is statuesque
Her timing is perfection
Her rhythm flows soulfully.
She is one graceful connection.

(By Neil Mckenzie)

"The Female Crooner"

In the early days of Big band and Swing,
And dancers were out there doing their thing,
There was a voice that could really croon.
It belonged to this girl,
She took you to the moon.
Her words were soft and a bit sensual,
When she moved to the music, it was very sexual.
Most men rose to see the occasion,
Most women shocked by her bold persuasion
A gift from god, she was sent from above?
Or an Angel here, just spreading the love.

(By Neil Mckenzie)

"Dianas Blessing"

Not quite sure where my Queen will end up today.
My heart yearns for her in the most passionate way
Her soul is free as it should always be.
I only pray that she is safe without the companionship
of me.
She is strong as her beautiful hair is long.
Let her make decisions with a forceful heir of
precision.
Let her stand proud.
Watch her soul shine through the cloud.
She has such a unique mind.
She definitly is one of a kind.
Stay strong my queen.

(By Neil Mckenzie)

"Foxes and Ravens"

With a world class body and veluptuous curves...
This smokin hot fox just stimulates all my nerves...
A form fitting black dress that caressed her thighs...
Makeup and jewelry that set off her eyes...
A natural hairstyle that glimmers and shines...
Maybe one day, she could truly be mine...
A perfect tan and well toned legs...
Come on baby...
Please dont make me beg...
A blue eyed raven with a heart of gold, as she
appeared before me she uplifted my soul...
I couldnt believe this vibrant creature was heading
toward me...
Once i layed eyes upon her it was all i could see...
She glided as she came across the room...
She smelled of flowers and expensive perfume...
She asked me my name and i said oh really?...
It must be a joke, then she sat down beside me...
She was drawn to me because of my inner light...
I said its ok sweetheart, enjoy it for the rest of the
night...
When she touched my hand, thats when i felt a
spark...

She was a lovely angel here to light up the dark...
Bold and seductive, from the heavens just for me...
A blue eyed raven who set my soul free...

(By Neil Mckenzie)

"The Natural Man"

The natural man, i do as i please and please as i do.
A very rare treat if he's
Got his eye on you
Built to have a lot of fun and tasked to get the job
done.
He speaks his mind.
But the words are never unkind.
More like a lesson for an uninformed mind
A great friend to have
And a philosopher of sorts.
He will always be there
Even if you aren't.

(By Neil Mckenzie)

"Mothers Day"

Mothers Day, we waited an entire year...
Mothers Day, a celebration of her life couldnt get any clear...
A strong woman who fought through all your vises...
A strong woman who bailed you out of every crisis...
Mom has been gone for a long long time...
But her love lives forever, in my heart and mind...
If your mother's still with you and hasnt made that trip...
Just talk to her and love her, because her time really goes quick.
But if its too late and you cant make that date...
Just get on your knees and pray to God...
Because he will look over his shoulder as "your" Mom gives him a nod...

(By Neil Mckenzie)

"Fathers Day"

"The Enchanted Forest" has existed for many years.
Its location moves from here to anywhere.
A small girl playing with her doll at the base of an old
tree.
She suddenly noticed the fairies eating raisins by her
knee.
"I wish my mommy and daddy didnt fight so much.
He hangs out at the local pub and he gets really
drunk.
He comes home in a rage that really scares us both.
Our lovely family used to be really close."
The fairies took note and dissapeared in a flash.
Their magic gave them a face, location and put the
father in a trance.
The first fairy appeared as the ultimate seductress.
"Sir would you come and help me with my new blue
dress?"
He eagerly followed her out the back door where the
other fairies appeared as hideous demon-like forms.
"A spell has been placed upon you that cannot be
removed.
If you dont straighten up your life, and dedicate
yourself to your child and wife you will be doomed."

The man sobered up quick and joined his family at home, where he never had another desire to drink or rome.

The little girl thanked the fairies for all they had done.

"No worries my friend it was actually a whole lot of fun and by the way...Happy Fathers Day.!!!"

(By Neil Mckenzie)

"The Soul of a Child"

Within her heart lays an angelic presence
It is innocent, truthful and part of her essence
The purpose of this soul is not completly known
But it has been there long before she was told
Somehow we need to nurture, care and teach this soul
So it will learn, thrive and break its mold
Full of love, hope and beautiful dreams
Perhaps she will lead us all to better things

(By Neil Mckenzie)

"Baby dont fear"

How do you know when she's the one?
She's the one we have all the fun
The girl who knows whats on your mind
She's your best friend all the way to the end
A beautiful soul thats kind
She will rock your world and still be that girl
That wipes your tears away
She will challenge your might without starting a fight
And then say i'm sorry all day.

(By Neil Mckenzie)

"Esperando a mi amor"

Clarita is home awaiting her man.
Her heart filled with anticipation for the touch of
Ariels hand.
As she thinks of him, her temperature rises.
Only he can satisfy this romantic crisis.
Their perfect love is what she craves.
So turn up the music and dim the lights.
Its time for Ariel to get busy tonite.

(By Neil Mckenzie)

"Amazing Grace"

When i was feeling down and there was no one else
around to lift my spirits and my hopes
She guided my steps and my eyes as my faded vision
would cause her to cry.
She always had hope that my eyes would get stronger
And not end up like our mother's
So she prayed for me and showed me the city
And maybe thats where god showed his pity
He placed his "Amazing Grace "upon the surgeons
hand...
I was blind but now I can see...
(thanks sis, by Neil Mckenzie)

"The Sucubus"

Watch out ladies she will steal your man.
All she needs is to place her fire in his hand.
When she enters the room all heads will turn.
If your love is weak, his heart will burn.
She collects your men and doesnt care how many she
gets.
Its the satisfaction of the hunt that cures her itch.
She is beautiful, charming and lovely to look at.
But if your love is weak...
This is what she seeks.
She feasts on the jealousy and anger that she can
cause.
To steal her best friends man?
There aint no law...
So look around ladies she may be closer than you
think....
So who just bought your man that drink?

(By Neil Mckenzie)

"The Magical Fairy"

When your spirits are low, thats when the magical
fairies will show.
They come from the land called "The Enchanted
Forest".
Each one has a name.
But the one that protects you will be the same.
They are michievous, fair and kind.
Sometimes they are nice, sometimes you have to pay
the price.
But they always try to give you peace of mind.
Dont try to control it, just follow her lead.
She was only summoned because you have a dire
need.
She see's the picture of your immediate future, not of
your long term dreams.
So give her your trust.
Its an absolute must.
She's a lot wiser than she seems.

(By Neil Mckenzie)

"Dont Trip"

Just because she looked at me...dont trip
Just because she talked to me...dont trip
I know her hair was fly, she had them big ole thighs,
what i say...dont trip
So she bought me a drink...dont trip
You saw her whisper in my ear...dont trip
All i could do was think about you, so baby...dont trip
So you think i'd cheat on you...right there?
You think i'd hook up with her...right there?
I know her eyes were nice and she smelled like spice
but baby...dont trip
She followed us home?...dont trip
Gonna wait till im alone?...dont trip
Like i said before you kicked me to the floor, baby...
dont trip
She owns a beauty salon...dont trip
She wants to sell you revelon...dont trip
I told you all i could do, was think about you so
surprise!..Happy Birthday

(By Neil Mckenzie)

"Oh, She So Naughty" (Part V)

I had a lot of things on my mind, and i really didnt have a whole lot of time...
So i took a little chance, when she asked me if i needed a dance...
I said sure whats the damage?....
She said 100 bucks a song and this wont take very long, And i guarantee you will lose that anguish...
Kind of expensive, but it sounded like fun...
So off to the couches for a run...
This better be good...
As the music began to play, this luscous body began to sway...
She slammed my drink, then chased it with a beer...
She looked me in the eyes and said hold on my dear...
She twerked me, as she jerked me, then she grinded me into the chair as she worked me...
She then grabbed my arms and compressed her thighs, until water was squirting out of my eyes...
She started to bounce and i mean really hard, all i could say was, oh my god !!!
She said shut up and concentrate, this aint no romantic kind of date...
When im done with you, i'll have pumped out everything you just ate...

She then turned around to smother me with her breast...
Thats when i whispered, "I think i need a rest"...
When the fun was done, and the smoke had cleared...
They found me passed out in the rear...
With a smile on my face...
From ear to ear...

(By Neil Mckenzie)

"Land of Rantell"

In the land of Rantell...
It's a beautiful frame of mind...
All your fantasys and desires are there for you to
admire...
Is she for real or just a lovely dream?...
A noble woman, sensual, beautiful...
And here to please...
I take her hand...
She places a kiss...
We hike through the valley of endless happiness...
We arrive at her "Meadow" full of love and desire...
Its time to pitch a tent and build on this fire...

(by Neil Mckenzie)

"Flight of the dancer"

Moves with such grace
All over the place
No move is wasted, no step is wrong
She trains all day to be the best
Her body poised to defeat the rest
Her routine is flawless in every way
Its sheer perfection that we witnessed today
We have been caught in her hypnotic trance
Theres no escape, theres no chance
She soars, she climbs,
She spins, she bends
As the flight of the dancer
Comes to an end
As we try to catch our breath again
Another flight is about to begin.

(By Neil Mckenzie)

"Mystery Girl"

With a beautiful smile and a touch of class, this sexy
lady is built for romance...
Those mysterious eyes, they lead to her soul...
This strong, shapely body is something to behold...
The way she walks is something to admire...
But its the way she talks, it sets your heart on fire...
I need a minute, just a little of your time...
To ask you...
"Girl, why you so fine?"...

(By Neil Mckenzie)

"The Healer's Sacrifice"

I will place my hands to keep you warm...
My soul will protect you from any harm...
You can put your trust completly in me...
My compassion for you is as strong as can be...
The pain in your shoulders, neck and thighs are only
temporary, i cant bare to see you cry...
My healing hands, i place upon thee...
I transfer the negative energy from you to me...

(By Neil Mckenzie)

"The Child"

In the land of the "Enchanted Forest"
The elves and fairies would sing in a perfect chorus.
They would stay busy all day, cultivating the plants
and flowers in May.
The mission of the dwarfs was caring for anything
that grew in the forest.
They were skilled farmers of sustaining all green life.
Then one day they heard crying across the way.
It was a child lost in the magic woods.
"I'm lost, hungry and scared.
And i cant find my mother anywhere".
The child began to sob.
Night was beginning to fall and the evil things would
crawl, hunting for anything they could consume.
The elves started to think, to the friendly Gnome we
must go.
And tomorrow we will take the child home.
That night the child ate raisins, plums, apples and
melons.
He fell fast asleep before he was done eating them.
The child was content.
The child was warm...
Then at the crack of dawn, there appeared a large
fawn.

"This will be your ride to take you to your mothers side.
So hold on tight and she will follow the fairies flight, they always seem to know the way to go"...
After a while a grateful mother and child were reunited at the forest edge.
The deer pranced away to avoid the excitement of people heading her way.
The mother turned around, just long enough to hear the sound of a perfect chorus eminating deep from within the "Enchanted Forest".

(By Neil Mckenzie)

"Fairies and Vampires"

Its a little known fact, but you may want to check.
If a vampire consumes the blood of a fairy, he will
have the power...
To walk at any hour...
And never fear the light of day.
Poor little fairy, she fell for the box of candy.
The vampires were about to move in for the kill.
Then she remembered she had her fairy flute and
began to play "A Sunrise For You".
Quite a distance away, the other fairies heard her play
and they knew instantly there was trouble.
So in one giant swarm they gave the appearance of
the Sun.
Appearing brighter and brighter as they grouped
together.
Then what the vampires thought they saw.
Was a magical flute that could summon the dawn.
So they took off to find the closest dark shelter.
Later that night, the Pixies feasted on fruits and
candy delights, and were all happy they saved the
little fairy.
The Enchanted Forest was at peace once again.

(By Neil Mckenzie)

"My Earth"

She is my temple my beautiful goddess I love her dearly as she gazes upon us She isnt perfect and she's not always right But i love her truly from morning, noon till night She makes my future as bright as the sun But i will settle for talk and a little fun She is my beacon that guides me through the day She is my Earth that grows fertile in every way (By Neil Mckenzie)

"Winged Tiger"

The queen was worried about her favorite fairy
She had been missing and started to query
She spared who she could to find her best friend
But it was the winged tiger who brought her home
safe again.

(By Neil Mckenzie)

"Time to Fight"

The queen cried "Im tired of running !!!"
She grabbed my axe and headed straight for the
woods
She raced to an area where the tall grass stood.
Silent and deadly like a big jungle cat.
She slashed and chopped until they all laid flat.
It was victories like these that were the hardest to
sieze.
But with the spirit of our queen
We always reigned supreme.

(By Neil Mckenzie)

"Setting the Trap"

Zeuss and Omar followed me at the rear
The queen and her winged tiger took to the air
Speed was of the essence to time this attack
Once we passed the mountains there was no turning
back
The dragons had left but the damage was done
They wiped out half an army and did it just for fun.

(By Neil Mckenzie)

"The Alliance"

My queen dressed in full battle gear
Watched as the dragon clan appeared
She had sought a secret alliance, with the creatures
who flew but were defiant.
They would protect the castle in everyway
But they would fight just for one day.

(By Neil Mckenzie)

"Warrior Queen"

I asked my queen where had she been?
I knew i broke a cardinal sin.
She looked at me with the windows of her soul
Protecting our kingdom is that too bold?
She wasnt alone in her quest to fight.
She took our pets, Tiger Left and Tiger Right.

(By Neil Mckenzie)

"The Day Your Heart Saw My Soul"

The day your heart saw my soul...
It was an emotion too hard for you to control
It was wrapped in an aura of pain...
It had a lock and a very large chain...
Your love would be the key for me...
It would set this prisoner's suffering free...
When i reached out you were already there
You broke that chain quickly, without a care
All that pain scattered like falling rain...
I asked you why? There was nothing for you to gain?...
You said my heart cried as it called your name...
You felt the bond that we were both the same...

(By Neil Mckenzie)

"She is a creature of the night"

A social butterfly.
They come to play games in the rays of the moon light.
Their smiles are infectous.
They can be so easy to please.
But in reality she's just a big tease.
Her mentality is a little different from me and you.
Her game is to seduce you, then toss you like an old shoe.
Its so much fun for her and her friends.
To watch you strike out, again and again.
Just when you think its a chance for romance.
She will fly away without giving you a glance...how annoying !

(By Neil Mckenzie)

"I Need To See You Naked..."

I need to see you naked...
You know what i mean...
I'm not talking about the flesh, among other things...
Tell me what makes you happy, and what makes
you mad...
Tell me what your
passion is, and what makes you sad...
Tell me about the dreams you have that make you cry...
Tell me about the truth that turned out to be just a lie...
You wear this "Front"...
An inpenetrable armour that's thick...
If i could hear the beat of your heart, that would
really do the trick...
But you distance yourself far enough that i cant feel
your soul...
I just want to be with you, not take control...
Just trust in me, as I do for you...
Our love will grow stronger...
This wont be hard to prove...
So drop that guard and let your soul breathe...
I'm waiting patiently...
I'm ready to see...

(By Neil Mckenzie)

"Anderson Fredricks"

With a soulful voice and a royal presence.
He commands the stage with a Motown Essence.
He will take you on a journey of all their hits.
From Smokey to Marvin, Stevie and the Temps.
His voice will take you higher, until you feel the fire
of all your favorite songs.
How can you go wrong
So enjoy this mans niche.
Because we call him Anderson Fredricks.
A singer you wont soon forget...

(By Neil Mckenzie)

Burning Man
"Spirit Willow"

In a post Apocolyptic world, we blame our nations
leaders for creating a nuclear swirl...
Those of us who barely survived joined the tribe
called the People to try and stay alive...
The once fertile lands were full of life and hope...
Are now vast deserts full of disease and drought...
A guide had to be chosen to lead us all the way...
To a land that could support the People and show us
all a better day...
It was "Spirit Willow" who could play the sacred
song...
She knew the rhythm of the region.
And the harmony just as strong...
She could communicate with nature, it lived in this
savage land...
She was our beacon of hope...
She was special to "Burning Man"...

(By Neil Mckenzie)

Never Forget
"September 11th"

As many years passed us by...
Never forget the ones who died...
Its about the unnessary death and tears of the loved
ones we left...
3000 deaths...
9000 wounded...
4 coordinated attacks.
The nation had recorded...
It caused all Americans to unite...
To get involved in this nations longest fight...
The axis of evil the heart of terrorism...
The military and first responders...
Countered with bravery and heroism...
Afganistan and Al Qaeda...
The evil ones who planned it all...
Maybe we need a guy like John Bolton...
To start the bombing and complete their fall...

(By Neil Mckenzie)

"Ukraine"

I would like you to do us a favor...
Just a little of your time and labor...
Just dig up some dirt i know it wont hurt...
For Mr. Biden...
He is just one of my friends...
I will give you the tools for this task...
I know its a lot to ask...
But i need this trash just like you need my cash...
I would like you to do us a favor...
I will send you Mr. Giuliani...
He likes to play in the dirt, he is loyal to me...
Just give him some time and he will twist it into a crime...
Crazy Rudy is one of a kind...

(By Neil Mckenzie)

"Christopher Columbus"

Christopher Columbus
Bringer of doom and mayhem...
Little did the Tainos know what misfortune he would bring them...
Rape and enslavement was his gift to the community...
They suffered and died because they had no natural immunity...
He forced them to dig for gold that the land couldnt yield...
As punishment, he chopped off their hands and tossed them into the fields...
Some of them fought to the death to avoid this slavery...
But a lot of them committed suicide just to get away from this tragic reality...

(By Neil Mckenzie)

"We are Better than This"

Grand Master Chump and his Legion of Doom...
Shaking up the house to give Putin some room...
Ukraine, Syria kicked like a can...
Patriotic diplomats fired cause they cant get with the
plan...
I rule this house...
You know I'm the man...
I will lie, cheat and steal if you dont believe i'm real...
Ok Pelosi, you busted me red handed...
But thats Ok, I'm the true American Bandit...
Because the first thing I stole as a world class
criminal...
Was America's pride and faith in anything
Congressional...

(By Neil Mckenzie)

"The Bad Daddy"

Public burnings, rapes and decaputations...
This was a madmans version of a psychotic nation...
A punk-ass bitch, the leader of Isis...
He totally folded when faced with a crisis...
He dragged his children into a tunnel with no exit...
He blew them all to Hell...
Special Forces, so persistant...
We chased him around the world for five long years...
Little did he know his end was so near...
Let us not forget this twisted cult still lives on...
Even though The Bad Daddy is dead and gone...
I hope his childrens souls were snatched from his
grip,
just before Bad Daddy made his final trip...

(By Neil Mckenzie)

Printed in the United States
By Bookmasters